Months
of the
Year

# December

by Mari Kesselring
Illustrated by Paige Billin-Frye

Content Consultant:
Susan Kesselring, MA
Literacy Educator and Preschool Director

# visit us at www.abdopublishing.com

Published by Magic Wagon, a division of the ABDO Group, 8000 West 78th Street, Edina, Minnesota 55439. Copyright © 2010 by Abdo Consulting Group, Inc. International copyrights reserved in all countries. All rights reserved. No part of this book may be reproduced in any form without written permission from the publisher.

Looking Glass Library™ is a trademark and logo of Magic Wagon.

Printed in the United States.

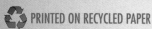 PRINTED ON RECYCLED PAPER

Text by Mari Kesselring
Illustrations by Paige Billin-Frye
Edited by Holly Saari
Interior layout and design by Emily Love
Cover design by Emily Love

**Library of Congress Cataloging-in-Publication Data**
Kesselring, Mari.
  December / by Mari Kesselring ; illustrated by Paige Billin-Frye ; content consultant, Susan Kesselring.
      p. cm. — (Months of the year)
  ISBN 978-1-60270-639-2
  1. December—Juvenile literature. 2. Calendar--Juvenile literature. I. Billin-Frye, Paige, ill. II. Kesselring, Susan. III. Title.
  CE13.K4724 2010
  398'.33—dc22
                              2008050710

The Year

Do you know

the 12 months of the year?

Are you ready to learn?

Then keep reading here!

What is the name
of the last month each year?
It is a time full
of holiday cheer.

It is December!

Was that your guess?

January  February  March  April  May  June

Let's learn about this month.
Then we can rest!

July    August    September    October    November    December

8

This month was the tenth month,
but there was a change.
December's month 12 now.
Isn't that strange?

On December 7, Pearl Harbor
was attacked long ago.
We listen to stories.
They're important to know.

December brings Christmas
and Hanukkah, too.
Plus Kwanzaa is this month.
There's so much to do!

Make time to help others.
Donate food and toys.
You will be spreading cheer
and holiday joy.

Why are snowflakes floating
down from the sky?
Winter starts in December.
I guess that is why!

CHECK OUT BOOKS HERE

It's Read a New Book month.

What fun!

Get a good stack.

You'll need more than one.

New Year's Eve
is on the very last day.
We are ready for a new year.
Hip hip hooray!

This year is over—
time for January once more.
Now you know the months.
You will get a good score!

# Find a New Book

December is Read a New Book Month. Find a new book to read this month. You can ask a librarian to recommend a good one for you.

# Learn a New Holiday

You probably have a December holiday that you celebrate every year with your friends and family. You might even have two! This month try to learn about a holiday that you do not celebrate. For example, if you celebrate Hanukkah, you could learn about Kwanzaa.

# Words to Know

**Christmas**—the Christian holiday that honors the birth of Jesus.

**donate**—to give something to other people as a kind gesture.

**Hanukkah**—a Jewish holiday that is also called the Festival of Lights. It lasts eight days.

**January**—the first month of the year. It comes after December.

**Kwanzaa**—the African-American holiday based on the African harvest festival.

**Pearl Harbor**—a military base in Hawaii that was attacked during World War II.

# Web Sites

To learn more about December, visit ABDO Group online at **www.abdopublishing.com**. Web sites about December are featured on our Book Links page. These links are routinely monitored and updated to provide the most current information available.